MW00625076

Issa's Best:

a translator's selection of master haiku

fur Michelle,

enjoy

By Kobayashi Issa

English translation by David G. Lanoue

David D. Lnoue

Copyright © 2012 David G. Lanoue

HaikuGuy.com

All rights reserved.

ISBN: 0985900369
ISBN-13: 978-0-9859003-6-6

CONTENTS

1 ABOUT THIS BOOK

This book has been twenty-six years in the making. In 1986 I began studying Japanese for the sole purpose of reading the haiku of Kobayashi Issa in its original form. By 1988 I had learned enough Japanese to begin translating Issa's one-breath poems to English. My first book, *Issa: Cup-of-Tea Poems; Selected Haiku of Kobayashi Issa*, came out in 1992; in it, I presented 450 haiku of Issa in seasonal order. In the year 2000 I launched my *Haiku of Kobayashi Issa* website, a searchable archive that at that time contained a database of 500 poems. Today that database has reached 10,000—a little less than half of prolific Issa's total output.

Issa: Cup-of-Tea Poems is now out of print, and though in 2009 I published a selection of 162 of his haiku in a bilingual English-Hindi edition published in India *(The Distant Mountain: The Life and Haiku of Kobayashi Issa)*, for a long time I have been contemplating the possibility of putting together a more substantial collection of Issa's haiku. While I intend to continue to offer all of the 10,000 poems that I have translated free to the world on the Internet, the present book is a guided tour through the work of Issa, gathering together in one text 1,210 of what I consider to be the master poet's most effective and evocative verses.

The book is divided into six sections. The first is "New Year's/Beginning of Spring." In the old Japanese calendar, New Year's Day was considered the first day of spring. It took place well over a month after our modern, Western New Year's Day. For Japanese haiku poets of the Edo period, New

Year's Day and the weeks following it—filled with sundry celebrations and rituals—was considered a season on its own. The next four sections—"Spring," "Summer," "Autumn" and "Winter"—contain haiku pertaining to these respective seasons. The final section offers a handful of Issa's haiku without seasonal references and, in one case, a haiku of mixed seasons that evokes both "blossoms" (associated with spring) and "moon" (associated with autumn). In this interesting poem, Issa transcends any single point in the cycle of the year to reflect, metaphorically, on his whole life and on life itself. In this section we also find some haiku about elements and animals that appear all year round, thus lacking any specific seasonal affiliation.

Because I don't want to clutter these pages with notes, I have selected haiku that can pretty much stand alone without commentary. However, if you happen to come across a reference unfamiliar to you, please visit my website to learn more at haikuguy.com/issa/.

2 ABOUT ISSA

The poet we know today as Issa was born on the fifth day of Fifth Month of 1763 (June 15 on the Western calendar) in Kashiwabara, a small village in the highlands of Shinano Province, today's Nagano Prefecture. His family name was Kobayashi; his given name, Yatarô. His father was a well-to-do farmer who owned enough land that the family's economic status, in the context of time and place, was closer to middle class than peasant. Yatarô's mother must have been warm and loving; he never recovered emotionally from her dying when he was three years old. He writes about her 47 years later, at age 50:

> my dead mother—
> every time I see the ocean
> every time...

His mother's replacement in the household, Satsu, soon gave birth to a son of her own, and treated young Yatarô cruelly, according to the latter's journal accounts, years later. For maternal love, he turned to his grandmother, but her death in 1776, when he was fourteen, was a second heart-crushing loss. The hostility directed at him by his stepmother Satsu disrupted domestic tranquility so much, Yatarô was sent away by his father to Edo, today's Tokyo, a year later. He was 15 years old in the Japanese age-reckoning system, according to which a person gains a year of age with each New Year's Day after birth. By Western standards, he was only thirteen. The historical record is silent on what type of servile or manual labor he found in Edo.

He joined the hordes of migrant workers from outlying provinces who swarmed every year into Edo to provide that city with a good portion of its labor force, surfacing in 1787 as a member of a haiku school led by Chikua: the Nirokuan. He eventually adopted the penname of Issa, "One Tea" or, more idiomatically, "Cup-of-Tea." The emotionally wounded, unwanted stepchild of the mountains had found poetry, or perhaps poetry had found him. Either way, he decided to dedicate his life to the way of haiku or, as it was called in Issa's day, *haikai*.

At age 29, inspired by the example set by the first great haiku master, Matsuo Bashô (1644-94), Issa took to the road on the first of a series of haiku-writing journeys. He describes himself in this period: "Rambling to the west, wandering to the east, there is a madman who never stays in one place. In the morning, he eats breakfast in Kazusa; by evening, he finds lodging in Musashi. Helpless as a white wave, apt to vanish like a bubble in froth—he is named Priest Issa."

"Priest Issa" visited his home village of Kashiwabara in Third Month of 1801, in time to find his father sick and dying. He tended to his father and vowed to him that he would stop wandering and return to live in the family homestead. According to Issa's poetic diary that covers this episode, *The Journal of My Father's Last Days* (*Chichi no Shûen Nikki*), stepmother Satsu and half brother Senroku rejected the death wish of their husband and father, respectively, and refused to allow Issa's return, thus setting off a long and bitter legal struggle. Finally, in autumn of 1813, the village headman decided that the Kobayashi house would be partitioned and that Issa would be permitted to live in one side of it. With great joy the poet moved in after 36 years of exile, and, two years later, married a local woman, Kiku. They proceeded to start a family of their own.

Much ink has been spilled about the ensuing tragedies that marred Issa's homecoming joy: four of his children dying, one by one, from diseases such as smallpox and, in one case, accidental suffocation. Especially devastating to the poet was the death of little Sato, his precious daughter, in 1819—a loss recounted in his journal *My Spring* (*Oraga haru*). Her death inspired one of his most poignant and famous verses:

> this world
> is a dewdrop world
> yes... but...

His wife Kiku's death in 1823 was another awful blow, but critics of Issa should beware of letting these family tragedies become the dominant theme when writing about him and his poetry. While he certainly mourns in his haiku, in times of mourning, he also laughs in times of laughter, gasps in moments of surprise...and so on. From his mid-twenties on, he was a prolific, dedicated writer committed to discovering the meaning of *all* of his moods—happy, sad, silly, reflective—in haiku. The image of him as a poet weighed down by "the sorrow of life" (to translate the title of one Japanese book about him) is grossly inaccurate.

Just as significant as the sorrows of this period of his maturity is the fact that his reputation as a teacher of haiku was spreading far and wide. Issa enjoyed great celebrity in his home province of Shinano, as well as in Edo and surrounding areas, where he visited from time to time. The period 1812 to 1824 represents the peak years of his poetry, but what kind of poetry was it?

He is known for four characteristics for which he was unrivaled by the other great figures of haiku tradition. The first is his warm, loving connection with living things, especially animals but also including humans and plants. As a Buddhist artist brimming with compassion and respect for his fellow beings, however small, Issa likes to address his nonhuman colleagues directly—a thing that prompts many critics to label him as a poet of "personification" or "anthropomorphism."

does the red dawn
delight you
snail?

In light of his Buddhist faith, however, he is not projecting "human" attributes on the snail—a fellow traveler on the road of existence. For Issa, even a snail can have a poet's heart that delights in the colors of the morning sky.

A second characteristic is his comedy. Issa perceives the ironic, the off-kilter and the absurd—and is prone to express such perceptions with the perfect timing of a master joke teller in his one-breath poetry. However, his comic approach should not be misunderstood as flippant or intellectually shallow. He rejects the tragic gesture of clinging to things, people, even to his own happiness—all of which must, inevitably, fade away. Instead, he approaches the universe with the comic gesture of not grasping: of letting go and surrendering to it with good humor.

the year's first rain—
my grass roof's
first leak

Though he often mentions his own poverty, referring to his home as a hermit's hut or a "Trash House" (*kuzu ya*), Issa accepts his situation, and all the rain that comes leaking in on New Year's Day. Some might worry or even weep in such circumstances; Issa chooses acceptance...and laughter.

A third characteristic of Issa is how he transforms the personal into art. He doesn't hesitate to tell the story of his life in his haiku. I've already mentioned his poems of mourning for lost loved ones that some readers and critics tend to overemphasize. His complete works include verses that relate all sorts of situations and moods in highly personal, intimately autobiographical statements.

> in hazy night
> stepping into water...
> losing my way

It was a hazy night of spring in 1795. In the uncertain, dreamlike light, Issa stepped off a path into water. We know from his travel journal that he was attempting to visit, that night, a friend and Buddhist priest, Sarai, who, he discovered, had been dead for several years. After being told of his friend's death, Issa begged Sarai's replacement at the temple for a night's stay, but was refused. He had come over 300 *ri* (1,178 kilometers), "without a soul to lean on, going over the fields and the yards..." In light of this biographical context, the phrase in the haiku, "losing my way," has deep, troubling resonance.

A fourth characteristic at which Issa surpasses all competition among masters of haiku is his propensity for defending the underdog, or at times, the under-frog.

> scrawny frog, hang tough!
> Issa
> is here

Issa's vision is democratic and often iconoclastic. His verses are filled with images of figures of authority in silly postures (a high priest of a temple pooping in a field) and reflections on the meaninglessness of human hierarchy and social class (a war lord or "daimyo" forced to dismount from his horse because of the higher power of...cherry blossoms!). This is why Issa is so loved by Japanese people. Bashô and Buson are perceived as revered masters of haiku sitting on high seats of honor; Issa stands shoulder-to-shoulder with common folk, shunning and lampooning authority and pretense.

looks like the boss
in the seat of honor...
croaking frog

As far as his biography goes, there are only a few more key
facts that the reader should know. In 1824, at age 62, he
married for a second time, briefly, but divorced within three
months. In 1826, he married his third wife, Yao. In 1827, his
house burned down in a fire that swept through Kashiwabara
village. He and his wife moved into a small, musty grain
barn—a structure that still stands today—where he died on the
19th day of Eleventh Month of the Tenth Year of the Bunsei
Era, the equivalent Western date being January 5, 1828.

In the mid-19th century, in 1851, Issa's poetic diary of 1819,
Oraga haru, was published with two postscripts that reveal how
he was perceived by his countrymen 24 years after his death. In
the first postscript, Seian Saiba mentions his humor but
hastens to add that "sarcasm is not the main object of this
priest; his writing also contains loneliness, laughter, and
sadness; and it expresses human feeling, worldly conditions,
and transience." The author of the second postscript, Hyôkai
Shisanjin, agrees: "Though it has a bit of jest in it, [Issa's
poetry] visits well the way of Buddhism...boldly not loathing
the dust of this world and filled with human feeling." Half-
hidden within his haiku jokes are profound and sincere
Buddhist lessons about worldly conditions and the transience
of things. This is how the generation after him viewed his
poetry.

In the more secular 20th century, the spiritual aspect of Issa's
writing gradually faded from the attention of critics, who chose
instead to dwell on biographical details, especially those details,
as I have mentioned, having to do with suffering and loss.
There were exceptions, of course: in 1969 Murata Shôcho
published a study of Issa in connection to Pure Land

Buddhism, *Haikai-ji Issa no geijutsu* (*The Art of Haiku Temple Issa*), a title derived from the verse:

> new spring
> Yatarô is reborn…
> into Haiku Temple

Yatarô, we remember, was Issa's given name. This poem celebrates his "rebirth" as a poet-priest, serving in the "temple" of haiku. My own book, *Pure Land Haiku: The Art of Priest Issa* (2004), continues in the tradition of Seian Saiba, Hyôkai Shisanjin, and Murata Shôcho in asserting that Issa is a spiritual poet for whom Buddhism and haiku are one thing.

Today, Issa is a world treasure. Though his popularity in Japan persists, with new books about him appearing every year, he is becoming just as recognized and admired in other countries, as more and more translations, like the present one, are published. He is a poet who speaks to our common humanity in a way that is so honest, so contemporary, his verses might have been written this morning. Bashô is the most revered of the haiku poets of Old Japan, but Issa is the most loved.

3 NEW YEAR'S/SPRING BEGINS

New Year's Day—
that I'm still on this journey
unbelievable

*

on New Year's Day
I have company
bird without a nest

*

homeless, too
seeing in the new year
in Edo

*

for them too
a New Year's feast...
pigeons, sparrows

*

celebrating New Year's
en masse...
rice field geese

*

on New Year's Day, too
standing "as is"...
trashy house

*

on New Year's Day
everywhere, a corrupt world's
blossoms

*

maybe this quake
will put the world right...
year's first day

*

New Year's Day—
in the dark before dawn
the lover cat

*

basking
in the New Year's sun...
my trashy hut

*

on New Year's Day
lucky! lucky!
a pale blue sky

*

around noon
New Year's Day begins...
little hut

*

a shiny-new year
has come again...
for my lice

*

a new year—
the same nonsense
piled on nonsense

*

another year
just taking up space...
thatched hut

*

from this year on
in my left hand, umbrella-hat
in the right, knapsack

*

turning into a child
on New Year's Day...
I'd like that!

*

First Month—
the plum trees blooming
elsewhere

*

my old coat—
a long First Month
creeps by

*

First Month—
instead of plum blossoms
a blizzard

*

First Month—
on the crossroads Buddha
a red skullcap

*

First Month—
even at the outcast's porch
plum blossoms

*

First Month, second day
the laziness
begins

*

First Month—
recording the cash spent
on sake

*

on the cat's grave
in First Month...
dried sardines

*

taking stock
of this old body...
spring's first dawn

*

my shadow too
in good health...
dawn of spring

*

crawl and laugh—
from this morning on
a two year old!

*

the nightingale's song
wonderfully strange...
spring's first dawn

*

in Amida Buddha
trusting...
spring's first dawn

*

spring's first dawn—
the priest pretending
to sweep

*

amazing—
in the house I was born
spring's first morning

*

even beggars toast
with sesame sake...
first of spring

*

my ramshackle hut—
just as it is...
spring begins

*

the samurai street
perfectly silent
spring's first dawn

*

once again
I've managed not to die...
blossoming spring

*

now with homeless eyes
I see it...
blossoming spring

*

with gums for grinders
greeting the blossoming
spring

*

at my gate
wildly it grows...
spring pine

*

all the windows
slid wide open...
Edo's spring

*

the nightingale comes
with his shadow...
spring window

*

my "Happy New Year!"
about average
my spring

*

spring begins—
I send up my smoke
like everyone else

*

the wild daisies
are celebrating...
spring's first day

*

we start the spring
in our everyday clothes...
me and the sparrow

*

"Spring begins"
just saying it...
green everywhere

*

the offbeat clomping
of clogs...
must be spring!

*

my province—
even the smoke
an ancient thing

*

spring's begun—
I even dream about
the grove of young pines

*

a new spring—
neither cow nor horse
has trod on it

*

new spring
Yatarô dies, priest Issa
is born

*

new spring
Yatarô is reborn...
into Haiku Temple

*

spring begins—
the obligatory
sparrows at the gate

*

spring begins—
more foolishness
for this fool

*

spring begins—
sparrows at my gate
with healthy faces

*

spring comes simply
with a pale blue
sky

*

stretching his neck
the turtle waits too...
the year's first day

*

in the storehouse
the hoe glinting...
year's first dawn

*

hole in the wall
pretty
my year's first sky

*

to the year's first sky
the lion-puppet
rears his head

*

the year's first sky
gives a gift...
snow flitting down

*

the year's first sky
hits a dead end...
Kazusa mountains

*

westward he prays
to the year's first sky...
priest

*

the year's first rain—
my grass roof's
first leak

*

big field—
my New Year's walk
follows holes made by canes

*

the cat considers
jumping up...
New Year's offering shelf

*

for drinking buddies
the usual New Year's pilgrimage...
sake shop

*

Mankind's Day—
from the main temple
the steam of bodies

*

plum blooming—
even hell's gate
CLOSED

*

this world of ours—
so fast the bonfires
burn out

*

homecoming servant—
tears precede everything
for the parents

*

yanking up a little pine
he says
a prayer

*

the puppy plays
hide-and-seek...
New Year's pine

*

fresh straw for the garden!
a sparrow dances
a black kite wheels

*

sending a "Happy
New Year!"
down the fox's hole

*

while taking
my morning piss...
"Happy New Year!"

*

secluded house—
even for the cat
a New Year's gift

*

the best New Year's
present!
her pink cheeks

*

on top
of the New Year's gifts...
cat curled asleep

*

New Year's present—
the nursing baby reaches
with little hands

*

how many times
a New Year's gift?
the fan returns

*

you've wrecked
my year's first dream!
cawing crow

*

while grasping
mama's breast...
the year's first smile

*

a beggar receives
alms, the year's first
laughter

*

first hot bath—
for my journey's lice
first sin

*

New Year's kite—
out of green leaves
then back in

*

today too, today too
the nettle tree snags
the kite

*

the trainer lets
his monkey hold it...
New Year's kite

*

New Year's Day—
a one-penny kite, too
in Edo's sky

*

a trendy kite soars—
below
a beggar's hut

*

with sooty paper
the stepchild's kite
easy to spot

*

clinging to the kite's
string...
the sleeping child

*

catching the kite's tail
with his mouth...
gargoyle

*

begging actors—
even the horse's rump
gets a blessing

*

in my province
even trained monkeys
wear noble hats

*

dancing monkey—
he gives his rice cake
to the child

*

the lion puppet
opens wide...
plum blossoms

*

are you coming down
crane, to see?
picking herbs

*

for each one picked
a puff on the pipe...
herbs

4 SPRING

the nightingale sings
with a country twang...
springtime

*

moon shining
on a one-penny bridge...
springtime

*

a crossroads sermon
gibberish
spring peace

*

spring peace—
Mount Asama's smoke
and the noon moon

*

spring peace—
a mouse licking up
Sumida River

*

spring peace—
a mountain monk peeks
through the hedge

*

pretty girls multiply
day by day...
spring days!

*

the chicken stares
at the man...
a long day

*

even for the meadow
butterflies...
the day is long

*

roly-poly pigeons
growing fatter...
a long day

*

in the long day
passing with mouth wide...
a crow

*

in the long day
they eat, they don't eat
pond turtles

*

a long day—
his account book serves
as a pillow

*

drawing eyebrows
on the white dog...
a long day

*

the crow, too
yawns and yawns...
a long day

*

long day—
the cow's slobber
about two miles long

*

a long day—
the dog and the crow
quarreling

*

a chicken strolls
through the sitting room...
a long day

*

the little owl
makes a face...
spring dusk

*

spring evening—
he comes out to pet
the gourd

*

forest ranger—
he sweeps away spring
with a broom

*

in a village
deep in the willows...
spring snow

*

from deep
in the lightning's flash...
spring snow falling

*

at my dinner tray
a sparrow chirps...
spring rain

*

walking along
a baking pan on his head...
spring rain

*

clang once more
mountain temple bell!
spring rain

*

my pine tree too
is grateful...
spring rain

*

spring rain—
ducks waddle-waddle
to the gate

*

the little shrine
is all azaleas...
spring rain

*

today too
looking at the same mountain...
spring rain

*

in the spring rain
a big yawn...
pretty woman

*

spring rain—
the uneaten ducks
are quacking

*

spring rain—
a mouse licking up
Sumida River

*

cheer up, owl!
the spring rain
is falling

*

spring rain—
he catches my yawn
dog at the gate

*

licking a bamboo leaf's
spring rain...
mouse

*

at morning market
he bares his chest...
spring rain

*

spring rain—
in the wife's sleeve
coins jingle

*

spring rain—
a child gives a dance lesson
to the cat

*

on the white blanket
of snow...
spring rain

*

pigeons mating
crows mating...
the spring rain falls

*

a day for wandering
a day for haiku...
spring rain

*

spring breeze—
the mop on the fence
drying

*

in spring's breeze
clutching chopsticks
the sleeping child

*

spring breeze—
a cow leads the way
to Zenko Temple

*

spring breeze—
where my feet are pointed
I'm on my way

*

his butt cooled
by the spring breeze
roof thatcher

*

spring breeze—
the great courtier
poops in the field

*

the puppy has caught
a mouse...
spring breeze

*

in spring breeze
his stole billowing...
a monk comes too

*

spring breeze—
monkey families, too
take healing baths

*

blown forth
by the spring breeze...
pilgrims

*

spring breeze—
three ride the same horse
home

*

spring breeze—
across the field a parade
of light blue parasols

*

spring breeze—
the priest gives his sermon
walking along

*

the spring moon
in a raindrop from the eaves...
falls again

*

in hazy night
stepping into water...
losing my way

*

for three pennies
nothing but mist...
telescope

*

lovers parting—
looking back at her house
until only mist

*

morning mist—
the castle's shutters
bang open

*

walking in mist
in a little sedge hat
with both parents

*

grilling sardines
in a mountain field...
thin mist

*

a precious harp
a beggar's flute
deep in mist

*

oh peach
come float to me!
spring mist

*

on a misty day
they chat...
horses in the field

*

misty day—
no doubt Heaven's saints
bored stiff

*

rap-a-tap
who's that coming
in the mist?

*

gambling in the field
a sermon in the thicket...
one mist

*

today too, today too
living in mist...
little house

*

waving umbrella-hats
farewell! farewell!
thin mist

*

misty day—
a hush in the big
sitting room

*

his attendants behind
haul the mist...
Lord Kaga

*

me and Buddha—
our heads
in the mist

*

paper umbrellas
dripping...
misty Kyoto

*

in thick spring mist
the burglar
laughing

*

the preacher's
hand gestures too...
lost in temple mist

*

heat shimmers—
how the cat talks
in her sleep!

*

heat shimmers—
the child's lost chicken
struts in the distance

*

vanishing
in the heat shimmers...
my humble hut

*

the goddess of spring
missed a few spots...
mottled mountain

*

in one spot
the crows congregate...
snow is melting!

*

snow melting
the village brimming over...
with children!

*

my hut—
the poverty-hiding snow
melts away

*

snow melting—
the thin children
of the slum

*

lovely—
in the leftover snow
both handprints

*

riddled with piddle
the last
snow pile

*

the stray cat
sharpens his nails...
last snow pile

*

on Amida Buddha's
temple clinging...
leftover snow

*

mother dog
testing the depth...
snow-melt river

*

the little tavern
open for business...
spring mountain

*

joining in
we curl to sleep too...
reclining Buddha

*

a confusing mix
of rain and snow...
spring equinox

*

in honor of the equinox
crawling into my sleeve...
a louse

*

a hundred miles to Edo
and his new job...
the child servant

*

even the sumo wrestler
has a blast...
Doll Festival

*

do you think
it's too smoky in here?
face of the doll

*

"Cousin Doll"
and "Grandchild Doll"
she names them

*

in one corner
soot-covered dolls...
husband and wife

*

giving her dolls
a good talking-to...
the child

*

the old doll
in the junk store window
sunning herself

*

herb cakes—
inside the mixing tub
a croaking frog

*

even tossing rice
is a sin...
sparring chickens

*

the mist covers up
the women first...
shell gathering

*

low tide
in a soft, soft rain...
darkness coming

*

my intrepid guide
on the low tide beach...
village dog

*

swinging on the swing
clutching
cherry blossoms

*

picking herbs—
on my coat a croaking
frog

*

led by a gang
of grannies...
the tea-picking song

*

the high priest
joins right in...
tea-picking song

*

where I saw
a pretty bird...
they burn the mountain

*

such is life—
the burning field's bugs
a feast for birds

*

make love, crows
while you can!
burning fields

*

crunch! crunch!
plowing the rice field
snow

*

mocking the farmer
plowing, the strutting
crow

*

the plowman lets me
cross his field...
temple pilgrimage

*

chrysanthemum garden—
one chop of the hoe
five cups of sake

*

the mountain crow
laughs at the branch
I grafted

*

wild cat—
after making love
he's the town pet

*

the lover cat
dandied up like Genji
at the hedge

*

cats' love calls—
between them flows
Sumida River

*

jumping so well
over the fire...
the love-crazed cat

*

a grain of rice
stuck to his nose...
lover cat

*

at daybreak
what grouchy faces...
Mr. and Mrs. Cat

*

so love-crazed
he even chases a chicken...
tomcat

*

fool cat
though tethered still crying
for love

*

the big cat
worn out from lovemaking
snores

*

mother cat
plays hide-and-seek...
with her kittens

*

the kitten
being weighed in the scales
keeps playing

*

mother cat
steals for her kittens...
run faster!

*

ten kittens
ten
different colors

*

on the shrine's altar
the buck offers
his antlers

*

baby sparrow—
even when people come
opening his mouth

*

sparrow babies
in plum blossoms
praise Buddha!

*

parent sparrows
baby sparrows...
a happy mountain

*

in the great bronze
Buddha's nose chirping...
sparrow babies

*

come and play
with me...
orphan sparrow

*

introducing their children
to society...
strutting sparrows

*

a troop of children
march behind her...
mother sparrow

*

baby sparrows
move aside!
Sir Horse passes

*

in and out
of prison they go...
baby sparrows

*

when you hold him kindly
he poops on you...
baby sparrow

*

baby sparrows
by the cow and the horse
untrampled

*

not hushing up
for the nightingale...
sparrows

*

the nightingale
wipes his feet...
on plum blossoms

*

nightingale
this fence is reserved
for you

*

a red berry
in its beak posing...
nightingale

*

the nightingale
drinks and bathes...
sewage canal

*

sing! sing!
off-key nightingale
at my window

*

nightingale—
his rain-drenched
morning voice

*

nightingale—
how many hundreds of songs
before you eat?

*

nightingale—
even strutting on the fence
a song

*

wafting through trees
a beggar's flute
a nightingale's song

*

a nightingale sings—
the east gate
of Amida's Pure Land

*

the nightingale
resigned to his fate...
voice in a cage

*

nightingale—
for the emperor too
the same song

*

no definite place
to spend the night...
evening swallow

*

from the great bronze
Buddha's nose...
a swallow!

*

renting a place
next door to the chickens...
swallows

*

the baby swallow's
flying lesson...
off the horse's rump

*

larks in the sky
people in the sea...
a holiday

*

down a narrow alley
the ocean...
a singing lark

*

coming down
to eat his lunch...
skylark

*

on a tiny island, too
plowing
to the lark's song

*

circling now and then
to eye the children...
skylark

*

farewell! farewell!
to the chicken...
the skylark flies away

*

its tail points
to the rising moon...
pheasant

*

a pheasant
loitering about, peeks
in my gate

*

as if it just spotted
a star
the pheasant cries

*

borrowing the buck's
back, the pheasant
cries

*

daybreak—
in a rooster-less village
a pheasant's cry

*

eating my rice
by lamplight...
the geese depart

*

geese fly north—
how they yearn to see
Mount Sarashina

*

departing geese
where will you moon-gaze
tomorrow?

*

just one
but he goes honking...
departing goose

*

the departing goose
drops an enormous
crap

*

traveling geese—
the human heart, too
soars

*

don't go geese!
everywhere it's a floating world
of sorrow

*

even the turtle
wants feathers...
the geese depart

*

after the big flock
silence...
geese flying north

*

resting his hands
on the green plum, asleep...
a frog

*

a fleeting moonlit
wedding night...
frogs singing

*

even in the well bucket
croaking all night...
a frog

*

sunset—
tears shine in a frog's eyes
too

*

next to my shadow
that
of a frog

*

get ready to see
my piss waterfall!
croaking frog

*

in every direction
ten thousand blessings...
croaking frogs

*

crossing the bridge
behind the blind man...
a frog

*

chin-deep
in the fallen blossoms...
a frog

*

facing every-which way
frog cousins
and second cousins!

*

serene and still
the mountain-viewing
frog

*

hitching a ride
on Mr. Turtle...
a singing frog

*

sitting in a row
peace on earth...
frogs

*

the little Buddha's head
a launch pad too...
frogs

*

scrawny frog, hang tough!
Issa
is here

*

in my hut
on urgent business...
a frog

*

locked in a staring contest
me...
and a frog

*

looks like the boss
in the seat of honor...
croaking frog

*

a frog squats
in his open palm...
a holy man

*

with a face
like he's contemplating the stars...
a frog

*

stone still
for the smelling horse...
a frog

*

dancing butterflies—
my journey forgotten
for a while

*

the year's first
butterfly
full of swagger

*

my hut
the butterfly's sleeping place
tonight

*

casting a spell
on the man...
meadow butterflies

*

gate after gate
making the rounds...
butterfly

*

flitting butterfly
to Buddha's lap
returns

*

such sweet harmony
to be reborn
a meadow butterfly!

*

clinging to
the boar hunter's arm...
little butterfly

*

butterfly dances
'round the arrow
in a dying deer

*

three feet
from the musket's barrel...
little butterfly

*

temple mountain—
a baby tumbles
a butterfly flits

*

from daybreak on
the butterfly couple
makes their living

*

amid butterflies
little butterflies
mountain home

*

stuck to the dog
curled asleep...
a butterfly

*

a butterfly
stuck fast to Amida
Buddha's cheek

*

blooming
with butterflies
the dead tree

*

"Follow me to Zenko Temple!"
a butterfly
flies

*

borrowing an antler
the little butterfly
rests

*

all day teasing
the horse's ear...
little butterfly

*

counting heads
in a hot tub...
little butterfly

*

festival day—
white monks
and a white butterfly

*

the butterfly's
soft landing...
in the tea kettle!

*

my arm
for its pillow
the butterfly sleeps

*

gambling in the field—
from the pot
a little butterfly

*

a previous life's bond?
little butterfly
on my sleeve, asleep

*

garden butterfly—
the child crawls, it flies
crawls, it flies...

*

renting a spot
next to the beehive...
sparrows

*

evening moon—
pond snails singing
in the kettle

*

the clam vomits
mud...
a moonlit night

*

O clams
meet the geese and gulls
of Greater Kamakura!

*

baby grass—
the stylish woman leaves
her butt print

*

solitude—
whichever way I turn...
violets!

*

flowering rape—
a soft seat
for the mouse

*

flowering rape—
and looking west
Zenko Temple

*

every tree
with its calling card...
spring buds

*

for the budding trees' spring
a little bird
gushes song

*

clobbered every day
by raindrops from the eaves...
camellias

*

a calf's face
stretches forward...
camellias

*

Kamakura—
who planted these camellias
in olden times?

*

lying on her back
sucking on the dangling
wisteria

*

one branch makes
Kyoto's sky...
plum blossoms

*

waiting so long
for just one branch...
plum blossoms

*

among the pines
all alone
a plum tree blooms

*

behind me
laughter at my rags...
plum blossoms

*

plum blossoms, moon
and the rump
of a cow

*

my hut's
down-and-out plum tree
has bloomed!

*

plum blossoms—
the sound of a three-penny
flute

*

unconquered
by the smell of broiled eels...
plum blossoms

*

plum blossom scent—
even the weasel passes
with a song

*

the pony's
favorite neck-scratcher...
blooming plum

*

plum blossoms—
spreading into the countryside
lice of Edo

*

on his scrap of mat
four or five pennies...
plum blossoms

*

in hell's mirror
the plum-blossom thief's
reflection

*

plum blossoms—
riding a dog
the Golden Boy

*

red plum blossoms—
on the porch
the bathed cat dries

*

Sir Toad
on a secret mission...
plum blossoms

*

plum blossoms—
in my account book I enter
"cash for sake"

*

the lazy dog
barks lying down...
plum trees in bloom

*

travel journal—
one moon
one blooming plum tree

*

plum blooming
even hell's cauldrons
CLOSED

*

the big horse
rubs his rump...
plum blossoms in the field

*

holy Jizo
stretch forth your hand!
plum blossoms

*

are you pointing out
these plum blossoms for stealing,
moon?

*

at the edge
of a stinking well...
plum blossoms

*

fluttering their way
into my head...
plum blossoms

*

by itself
my head bows...
plum blossoms!

*

even for the god
of the outhouse...
plum blossoms

*

when plum trees bloom
hot tubs
overflow

*

he leaves the outhouse
unlatched...
plum blossoms!

*

plum blossoms—
dried sardines scattered
on the cat's grave

*

have celestial maidens
descended to earth?
blossom clouds

*

that temple bell
sounds like Ueno's...
clouds of blossoms

*

evening—
a bird of prey flies home
into blossoms

*

from where
did those blossoms float?
Sumida River

*

eating my pickle
rind and all...
blossom shade

*

in falling rain
one man remains...
blossom shade

*

cherry blossoms—
I've been living in Edo
for this day!

*

rain of cherry blossoms—
this year, too
I've sinned

*

is even the beggar
singing a song?
blossom shade

*

splish-splash
the sparrow takes
a blossom bath

*

simply trust!
cherry blossoms flitting
down

*

to be alive like this
is a wonder...
blossom shade

*

among cherry blossoms
a long stay
in this world

*

in falling blossoms
growling to Amida Buddha...
temple dog

*

squirming
through the cherry blossoms...
people

*

in this world
over hell...
viewing spring blossoms

*

tucking himself in
under fallen blossoms
puppy

*

blossoming mountain—
come out and play
devil in me!

*

like me
no good at dying...
blossoms at the gate

*

all morning
to the falling blossoms...
my farts

*

cherry blossoms—
playing the dandy, in my mouth
an empty pipe

*

cherry blossom shade—
no one an utter
stranger

*

he sneaks up
to my thatched hut
for blossom viewing

*

treating my thatched hut
like home...
blossom viewers

*

young folk beat us
to the spot!
blossom shade

*

all the nondrinkers
seem gloomy...
blossom shade

*

the temple blossoms
without struggle
fall

*

blossoms become clouds—
people become
smoke

*

cherry blossoms—
the pretty women of Kyoto
cheeks wrapped in scarves

*

Edo voices—
the blossom viewing ends
in a quarrel

*

in ceremonial robe
he's fallen down drunk...
blossom shade

*

fussing, fussing
in the blossom shade...
gamblers

*

carrying his mother
and leading his child by the hand...
cherry blossoms!

*

"No soldiers
allowed!"
say the cherry blossoms

*

the home village
I abandoned...
cherry trees in bloom

*

blown to the big river
floating away...
cherry blossoms

*

though my rice sack
is empty...
cherry blossoms!

*

on Mount Ubasute
where the old were left to die...
cherry blossoms

*

all night
under the cherry blossoms
nagging

*

under the cherry tree
in bloom
a little gambling shack

*

even the frog's eyes
can't turn away...
cherry blossoms!

*

the puppy is escort
on the pilgrimage...
cherry blossoms!

*

the devil's horns
snap off!
cherry blossoms

*

the roof sweeper
stands still...
evening cherry blossoms

*

the cherry blossoms fall—
I apologize to a dog
in passing

*

the cherry blossoms
that stirred me, shade me
no more

*

the lost child
clutches them tightly...
cherry blossoms

*

remote province—
even in a haunted place
cherry blossoms

*

lord of the mountain's
cherry blossoms...
stone Buddha

*

from Japan's
front door on...
cherry blossoms!

*

a hot bath
a prayer
then cherry blossoms!

*

praise Buddha!
sleeping in the light
of cherry blossoms

*

granny comes too
led by a cow...
cherry blossoms

*

sticking to
her stick of candy...
cherry blossoms

*

the war lord
forced off his horse...
cherry blossoms

*

without you—
how vast
the cherry blossom grove

*

trickling from
a village child's sleeve...
cherry blossoms

*

pouring onto
the faces of sinners...
cherry blossoms

*

Lucky the Toad, too
swaggers out...
peach blossoms

*

the horse stands
rubbing his rump...
peach blossoms

*

dangling in
the yellow roses
the bull's balls

*

holding up
the hazy moon...
willow tree

*

an evening spot
for calling fireflies...
planting a willow

*

dawn's glow
even more of a wonder...
willow tree

*

lined up
with the evening mountain...
a willow

*

killing a chicken—
the willow at the gate
so green

*

from the willow
a ghost attacks!
the child

*

the sleeping puppy
paws
at the willow

*

shrouding his rear
as he poops in the field...
a willow

*

with one gust
it becomes the perfect
willow

*

the pony
has crept
through the willow

*

when night falls
whores tug at sleeves...
willow tree

*

to the old woman
doing laundry, the evening
willow bows

*

water rising—
the shrimp crawls up
the willow

*

peeking out
from the willow tree...
face of a fox

*

swish-swish
spring is departing...
field of grass

5 SUMMER

summer dawn—
riding an ox, asleep
the hay cutter

*

stitching together
the short summer nights...
singing frogs

*

in the short summer night
wriggling to climax...
maiden flowers

*

"Dawn's coming quick!"
cries the town crier...
sparrow

*

short summer night—
in the field turtles
cavort

*

scowling
at the hot night...
gargoyle

*

hot day—
the cool abacus
for a pillow

*

ink-stained hands
sweaty face...
the child's calligraphy!

*

hot night—
bats dangle
at the river's edge

*

hot day—
a staring contest with
a gargoyle

*

cool air—
the half moon moves
across a puddle

*

drip-drip
goes the cool water...
the bees are gone

*

cool air—
a dark little nook
on Sumida River

*

in summer cool
ambling down my road
to hell

*

cool air—
the shape of the cloud
is Buddha

*

it's a down, down
downtrodden land...
but cool!

*

lying spread-eagle
cool
lonely

*

the number one
best cool breeze...
outhouse

*

evening cool—
tossing water on the
horse's rump

*

cool air—
even in my soup bowl
Mount Fuji!

*

in the cool air
slap! slap! his hair is combed...
Sir Horse

*

in summer cool
the account book
for a pillow

*

summer cool—
the gate to Buddha's
Pure Land

*

cool breeze—
she eats with an appetite
for two

*

cool air—
the sound of well water
drawn at night

*

cool air—
straight from the holy grove
it comes

*

cool air—
paper snowflakes fluttering
down

*

cool air—
my wife chases a mosquito
with a spoon

*

becoming demons
becoming Buddhas...
the midsummer clouds

*

this rain
a greeting card from heaven...
midsummer heat

*

is the wind
on summer vacation?
grassy field

*

rainy season—
a crab strolls into
the big sitting room

*

all day, all day
day after day...
Fifth Month rain

*

two won't fit
in the little shrine...
Fifth Month rain

*

crushed
under the Fifth Month rain...
my home

*

Fifth Month rain—
not a rock
without azaleas

*

in Fifth Month rain
splish-splash the strutting
crow

*

in the thicket shade
he sharpens his sickle...
Fifth Month rain

*

Mr. Toad's
sour Buddha face...
Fifth Month rain

*

a servant in Zen meditation
faces a wall...
Fifth Month rain

*

just for fun
into the hot tub I go...
Fifth Month rain

*

what a face
this frog is making!
Fifth Month rain

*

vines today
morning-glories tomorrow...
Fifth Month rain

*

go, horsefly
through the ripped paper door!
Fifth Month rains are over

*

rainstorm—
a beggar with his potted
pine

*

like he's snapping
at the downpour...
gargoyle

*

now the cloudburst
only a pitter
patter

*

watching the downpour
under a temple
bell

*

darting to the beat
of the downpour...
a swallow

*

standing dead center
in the downpour...
a blind man

*

rainstorm—
a naked rider
on a naked horse

*

stillness—
in the depths of the lake
billowing clouds

*

billowing clouds—
have the pine trees
shrunk a bit?

*

patting my belly
full of worms...
billowing clouds

*

the swimming flea
thinks to reach them...
peaks of clouds

*

the ants' road
from peaks of clouds
to here

*

less high
than the sins of men...
peak of a cloud

*

in soup kettle
and outhouse
the summer moon

*

summer mountain—
with each step more
of the sea

*

the beehive dangles
heavily above...
pure water

*

from the shade
of the poison plant...
pure water

*

through a village of people
the water no longer
pure

*

evening shadows—
he throws pure water
on the horse

*

touching the princess lily's
heart...
pure water

*

green rice field—
grabbing the chopsticks
he watches

*

if my father were here—
dawn colors
over green fields

*

KOBAYASHI ISSA

an arm for a pillow
imagining the green rice field
is mine

*

your rice field
my rice field
the same green

*

at the dinner
tray's edge...
a green rice field

*

Buddha's birthday—
fat little sparrows
and their parents

*

the Buddha
even in beggar-town
is born

*

horseflies' and bees'
big lucky day...
Buddha's birthday flowers

*

the ants rush
to make a road...
Buddha's birthday flowers

*

summer seclusion—
every night the toad
comes calling

*

little snail
inch by inch, climb
Mount Fuji!

*

in the outcasts' village
easily overlooked...
summer banners

*

from holy Jizo's
holy neck it hangs...
rice dumpling

*

dangling from
the little boy's neck...
a rice dumpling

*

the kitten unwraps it
with clever paws...
rice dumpling

*

the dragonfly, too
works late...
night fishing

*

after a scolding
the weary cormorants
dive again

*

the whole town sleeps
while the cormorants
toil

*

outdoing the cormorant
in skillful imitation...
a child

*

weary cormorant—
no festival holiday
for you

*

today too
today too...
cheating clouds

*

sweat drops from cows
from horses...
blades of grass

*

also changing
into a summer robe...
my journey's lice

*

doing what I can
to shrink the belly...
new summer robe

*

the dandelion gives
a nod...
my new summer robe

*

just today
I wish I had neighbors...
my new summer robe

*

when I'm dead
who'll wear it next?
new summer robe

*

his father's
father's father wore it too...
summer robe

*

called a crybaby
she starts crying...
summer kimono

*

the high priest
poops in the field...
parasol

*

old priest—
even while plucking grass
a parasol holder

*

the cat naps
in a lacquered tray...
summer room

*

stopping to count
my mosquito net's holes...
sickle moon

*

no divine punishment yet—
napping
under the net

*

sleeping in new
mosquito nets...
horses of Edo

*

tomorrow night and the next
the same...
in my mosquito net, alone

*

Osaka—
on the back of an ox
a siesta

*

spread-eagle arms
legs opened wide...
siesta

*

like the humans
a monkey too
curled up for siesta

*

such a moon!
yet he's under his fan
asleep

*

in the darkness
swishing, swishing...
paper fan

*

singing a song
and slapping his butt...
with a fan

*

the little pilgrim
being led by hand...
red paper fan

*

top to bottom
the mouse eats
the fan

*

with my wastepaper fan
striking poses...
alone

*

stroke victim—
even holding a paper fan
an ordeal

*

the big cat
flops down to sleep
on the fan

*

with a face
come down from heaven
she is fanning

*

in the pauses
of our pillow talk
fanning

*

smoking out mosquitoes—
soon the fireflies
are gone too

*

calling down—
from deep in the well
an answer

*

a popular song—
from the bottom of the well
he joins in

*

evening cool—
the toad who comes out
I call "Lucky"

*

a soot-grimed Amida Buddha
at my side...
evening cool

*

in a remote village
they're used to poverty...
evening cool

*

the fish in the tub
won't know tomorrow...
evening cool

*

a wifeless man
makes his plants bloom...
evening cool

*

a farting contest
under the moonflower trellis...
cool air

*

with a kitchen knife
choosing eels...
a cool evening

*

massaging my back
with the pine tree's gnarl...
evening cool

*

evening cool—
with my feet counting
the mountains of Shinano

*

scowling
at the cool night...
gargoyle

*

naughty child
though tethered enjoys
evening's cool

*

scooping up the ocean
in my hands...
evening cool

*

lighting my pipe
with an incense stick...
cool air

*

banging the temple gong
just for fun...
cool air

*

one horsefly
on the horse's belly
cooling off

*

evening cool—
the great high priest
tells jokes

*

father and son's
fart contest...
cool air at the gate

*

hidden in trees
praising Amida Buddha...
rice planter

*

my rice field too
song by song
is planted

*

when your village is done
where next?
rice-planting umbrella-hat

*

even worthless me
is invited...
rice-planting sake

*

the child on her back
cries to the beat...
rice-planting song

*

rice-planting girl—
on her back a butterfly
sleeps

*

growing up
with the bush clover...
a fawn

*

following behind
the hunter with his bow...
a fawn

*

growing up
in the thick of chickens...
a fawn

*

get a move on, bat!
it's dinnertime
in Kyoto

*

moon at the gate—
the mosquito-eating bats
prosper

*

like the bats
night's streetwalkers too
make their slow rounds

*

from the arms
of the Deva Kings
bats dangle

*

generations of bats
have called this storehouse
home

*

flood waters—
bats dangle
from the crossing-rope

*

daybreak—
the rooster-less village
has a cuckoo!

*

I've waited long
for thee
O cuckoo!

*

is the night this nice
in China?
cuckoo

*

a cuckoo—
the bridge beggar
listens too

*

worthy of Sir Cuckoo—
the moon
in the pine

*

how many gallons
of Edo's rain did you drink?
cuckoo

*

don't choke
on the hermit's pipe smoke!
cuckoo

*

are you trying not to
look at my hut?
cuckoo

*

"That's a poor excuse
for rain!"
sings the cuckoo

*

the cuckoo hurls threats
at the horse
passing by

*

little cuckoo
sing! sing!
Issa is here

*

of all the gods
which ones are real?
cuckoo

*

from today on
let no one out-sing you!
Edo cuckoo

*

crawling across a bridge
far below...
"Cuckoo!"

*

in this darkness
don't get your nose picked!
cuckoo

*

in heavy rain
seething with resentment
cuckoo

*

looking askance
at the great lord's fortress...
cuckoo

*

the cuckoo serenades
all of Edo
all...night...long!

*

sing soft!
a samurai lives next door
cuckoo

*

in a previous
life, my cousin?
mountain cuckoo

*

like warbling pure haiku
mountain
cuckoo

*

the mountain cuckoo sings
at Mr. Toad's
funeral

*

does the caged
nightingale hear?
mountain cuckoo

*

admonishing
my heavy drinking...
mountain cuckoo

*

cheered on
by a reed thrush
the incompetent thief

*

just one reed
for the reed thrush...
Sumida river

*

reed thrush
on a bamboo stalk's
tippy-top

*

the village hits
a crescendo of snores...
reed thrush

*

to the rhythm
of a moorhen's cries...
a cloud speeds by

*

with skin peeled off
snake
are you cool?

*

on Buddha's lap
a snake's forsaken
garment

*

lightning flash—
the toad
rubs his head

*

looking like
"I can ride the mist"...
a toad

*

with that mouth
he could vomit a cloud...
toad

*

"Allow me to present myself—
I am the toad
of this thicket!"

*

the horse's fart
wakes me to see...
fireflies flitting

*

my house
where the town's fireflies
hide out

*

is my wrinkled hand
bad for walking?
first firefly

*

sparkling fireflies—
even the frog's mouth
gapes

*

they have kids—
the bridge beggars
calling fireflies

*

a night of fireflies
has arrived...
my spring-planted willow

*

a mouth calling fireflies—
one
flies in

*

the dog sparkling
with fireflies
sound asleep

*

sweeping them off
the cow's back...
fireflies

*

guiding the way
to firefly-viewing...
the hut's dog

*

do you think
my hair's a thicket?
firefly

*

naughty child
though tethered calling
fireflies

*

on my sleeve
catching his breath...
worn-out firefly

*

flitting firefly—
uncaught by the hand
uncaught again!

*

though wrapped in
tissue paper...
a firefly's light

*

evicted
from the sunset bell...
firefly

*

secluded house—
a firefly
resort

*

blown away
by the horse's fart...
firefly

*

house in deep shade
at high noon...
fireflies

*

after the bath
tickling my armpit...
firefly

*

one cocoon
in the stone Buddha's
lap

*

why is playing
with fire such fun...
tiger moth?

*

big caterpillar—
into the ants' hell
it has fallen

*

mosquito larvae—
in a day how many
ups and downs?

*

a celebration—
the mosquitoes of Kazusa
feast on me too

*

from deep inside
the pretty flower...
a mosquito

*

evening sky—
the whine of mosquitoes
pretty

*

through a hole
in the mosquito swarm...
Kyoto

*

my home—
for the mosquitoes
a famous resort

*

my home
where I even exhale
mosquitoes

*

on a blade of grass
the mosquito
plays dead

*

driven from next door
here they come...
mosquitoes

*

swatting a fly
but hitting
the Buddha

*

while swatting a fly
"All praise to Amida
Buddha!"

*

while I'm away
enjoy your lovemaking
hut's flies

*

fly on my umbrella-hat
from today on
a citizen of Edo!

*

one man, one fly
one large
sitting room

*

living long
the flies, fleas, mosquitoes...
a poor village

*

the old hand
swats a fly
already gone

*

gaping mouthed
and fly-hungry...
dog at the gate

*

don't swat the fly!
praying hands
praying feet

*

swat! swat!
the escaping fly buzzes
with laughter

*

where there's people
there's flies
and Buddhas

*

swarming flies
how do my wrinkled hands
taste?

*

I go back in
my thatched hut...
the fly does the same

*

"It's a good year!"
they buzz...
flies at the gate

*

on the high priest's
head...
flies making love

*

the bell of life passing—
oh flies and worms
listen well!

*

in a sake cup
a flea
swimming! swimming!

*

a flea jumps
in the laughing Buddha's
mouth

*

evening—
in a big sake cup
moon and a flea

*

pesky flea
caught in my hand
become a Buddha!

*

dawn—
to Fuji! to Fuji!
fleas jumping off

*

though it's cramped
practice your jumping
hut's fleas

*

the mouth that gnawed
a flea:"All praise
to Amida Buddha!"

*

she counts flea bites
while her child
suckles

*

if you jump flea
jump
on the lotus

*

a new tatami mat—
fleas jumping
bumpity bump!

*

into the big river
tossing her lice...
pretty woman

*

do you also miss
your mother?
cicada

*

the dog turns
in the cicada's direction...
mouth agape

*

go ahead, make love!
make love!
summer cicadas

*

temple mountain—
buzzing into my sleeve
a cicada

*

summer cicada—
even in his lovemaking break
singing!

*

the cicada chirrs
on the grazing horse's
cheek

*

little monk—
deep in his sleeve
singing, a cicada

*

so many cicadas
singing and tumbling off...
umbrella-hat

*

all the baby spiders
scatter
to make a living

*

at my feet
when did you get here?
snail

*

does the red dawn
delight you
snail?

*

morning rain—
look! next to me
a snail

*

just as you are
become Buddha!
snail

*

in evening moonlight
going bare-chested...
snail

*

the brushwood door's
substitute lock...
a snail

*

little snail, no different
asleep
awake

*

closing the door
he drops off to sleep...
snail

*

taking a siesta
with the farmer...
a snail

*

blowing her snot
on the moonflower...
a young girl

*

blowing her snot
on the moonflower...
granny

*

just being alive
I
and the poppy

*

words
are a waste of time...
poppies

*

speaking
this day's deepest thoughts...
poppies

*

carrying a poppy
he passes through
the quarrel

*

the peony falls
spilling out yesterday's
rain

*

the cat's bell tinkling
in the peonies
here and there

*

by itself
my head bows...
peony!

*

sitting on her eggs
the chicken admires
the peony

*

a masterly climb
to the top of the peony...
frog

*

lotus blossoms—
the beggar's smoke
wafts over

*

Lucky the Toad
crawl out!
lotus blossom

*

in a place
where no light flickers
the perfect lotus

*

blooming lotuses
where sewer water
pours

*

after feasting on people
the horsefly mounts
the lotus

*

holy Jizo
in the blooming pinks...
dead center

*

the young buck's
mouth can't reach...
the iris

*

where piss dribbles,
dribbles down...
irises

*

thatched roof—
the irises piercing it
bloom

*

staring at me
on and on...
toad in the lilies

*

from today on
hear my "Praise Buddha!"
lilies

*

dangling from
the young buck's antler...
lilies

*

evening gloom—
a fawn's spots
in the lilies

*

on the duckweed's softness
the frog's
picnic

*

Sir Mouse
nimbly, nimbly crosses
the duckweed

*

lording over
the black barley ears...
village dragonflies

*

over me
soon enough you'll bloom
moss blossoms

*

in holy Jizo's
lap, eyes, nose...
blooming moss

*

while I was away
just for a while...
a splendid young bamboo!

*

becoming a walking stick
little bamboo
at the peak of youth

*

staring at the shoots
of new bamboo...
Buddha

*

bamboo shoots—
big brothers, little brothers
growing up

*

bamboo shoots—
a woman digs them up
like a dog

*

"Grow, grow, grow
melons!"
buzz the bees

*

if someone comes
change into frogs!
cooling melons

*

first melon of the season
in her grasp...
sleeping child

*

my hut—
the only cooling melon
is the moon

*

fresh new leaves—
the cat and the crow
quarrel

*

the holy man
grabs a siesta...
grove of summer trees

*

hearing voices
the leech drops...
summer trees

*

in deutzia blossoms
the priest buries
the frog

*

deutzia blossoms—
the children play
funeral

*

with deutzia blossoms
on this lucky day...
outhouse

*

the deutzia blossoms
light up
my lap

*

deutzia in bloom
the children make
mud-dumplings

*

deutzia blossom hedge
the dog's
maternity room

*

thorn hedge—
the dog crawls through
like a pro

*

even wild roses
of a downtrodden land
reach enlightenment

6 AUTUMN

autumn begins—
I thought by now this journey
would've ended

*

"Autumn's begun"
just saying it
I feel cold

*

not knowing that
autumn's begun, puppy
Buddha!

*

nippy weather—
the meaning of "parent"
sinks in

*

morning cold—
the toad's eyes too
open wide

*

out of sake
such is my life...
a cold night

*

his grinding teeth
wake me...
a cold night

*

a pounding pestle
completes the scene...
a cold night

*

twisting the chicken's
neck...
a cold night

*

for the neighing horse
the cold night
same as for me

*

one and all
faces of the Buddhas
cold tonight

*

brazenly
the mouse sneaks in...
a cold night

*

practicing calligraphy
on my belly...
a cold night

*

another year closer
to sixty...
the cold night

*

feeling for the stone bridge
with my feet...
a cold night

*

my knees
this cold night in the mountains
feel older

*

going outside the fence
to fart...
a cold night

*

one by one
even the cats come home...
cold nights

*

looking up, wrinkles
looking down, wrinkles...
a cold night

*

the katydid
cranks up the volume...
a cold night

*

dyeing the hands
indigo blue...
the cold night

*

"A man"
is registered at the inn...
a cold night

*

practicing writing
in the tray's ashes...
a cold night

*

"Here's the outhouse!"
the horse calls...
a cold night

*

the stomped-at mouse
squeaks with laughter...
a cold night

*

at the window
insects too
a cold night huddle

*

crabs jamming themselves
in the cattails...
autumn night

*

yet another traveler
overtakes me...
autumn dusk

*

oh snail
how do you make your living?
autumn dusk

*

quite remarkable
being born human...
autumn dusk

*

the little monkey
chews on a pipe...
autumn dusk

*

the pony also
sets off on a journey...
autumn dusk

*

another year
I didn't die...
autumn dusk

*

I too
without a home...
autumn dusk

*

I know this wall scribbler's
name...
autumn dusk

*

the only one to nag now
is the wall...
autumn dusk

*

autumn evening—
a traveling man busy
stitching

*

autumn evening—
from elsewhere another horse
neighs in reply

*

autumn evening—
a little hole in the window
blows flute

*

"It's a foolishly long
night!" I say
in the long night

*

wooden clogs
clomp! clomp!
a long, weary night

*

going out to fart
about ten times...
a long night

*

for you fleas
the night must be long...
and lonely?

*

looking pretty
in a hole in the paper door...
Milky Way

*

sleeping mat—
blowing pipe smoke
at the Milky Way

*

in cold water
sipping the stars...
Milky Way

*

in my sake cup
down the hatch!
the Milky Way

*

frost has formed
on the futon...
Milky Way above

*

hey boatman
no pissing on the moon
in the waves!

*

the defeated wrestler, too
joins the crowd...
bright moon

*

which of you owns
that red moon
children?

*

granny walks along
drinking sake...
a moonlit night

*

the turtle and moon
merge...
Sumida River

*

old wall—
from whichever hole
autumn moon

*

harvest moon—
when my heart's had its fill
it's dawn

*

in some sky
rain isn't falling...
harvest moon night

*

under my bottom
the stone warms up...
moonlit night

*

lit by the harvest moon
no different...
trashy house

*

trying and trying
to grasp the harvest moon—
toddler

*

harvest moon—
going out
going back in

*

amazing—
in the house I was born
seeing this moon

*

harvest moon
on the mountain scarecrow's
sleeve

*

guard my hut's key
pine tree!
going moon gazing

*

the sake gone
time to buckle down
and moon-gaze

*

harvest moon—
fifty-seven years
of traveling autumns

*

harvest moon-gazing
priests, samurai
merchants

*

harvest moon—
digging in the teacup
for sake money

*

harvest moon—
some are stretched out
some praying

*

on harvest moon night
greeting the moon...
with snores

*

if only she were here
for me to nag...
tonight's moon!

*

a farting contest—
harvest moon night
in the hut

*

the sold pony
looks back at mother...
autumn rain

*

oh snail
how do you make your living?
autumn rain

*

the horse drinks
medicine too...
autumn rain

*

my evicted fleas
have returned...
autumn rain

*

one by one
everyone has left...
autumn wind

*

autumn wind—
a beggar looking
sizes me up

*

autumn wind—
the cicadas' grumbling
is louder

*

in autumn wind
trusting in the Buddha...
little butterfly

*

behind me
the autumn wind blows
me home

*

under which star
is my home?
autumn wind

*

through what teeth
I have left
autumn's wind whistles

*

autumn wind—
landing on my belly
a katydid

*

autumn wind—
Issa's heart and mind
stirring

*

in autumn wind
escaping on foot...
firefly

*

will these old knees
journey on?
autumn wind

*

in the autumn wind
clutching my sleeve...
little butterfly

*

in autumn wind
a homeless crow
is blown

*

autumn wind—
red flowers she wanted
to pick

*

eating my rice
in solitude...
autumn wind

*

blowing two people
after their fleas...
autumn gale

*

just the other day
we said goodbye...
dewy grave

*

in beads of dew
one by one my home
village

*

happily watching
the dewdrops forming...
a frog

*

in the silver dewdrops
vanishing...
my house

*

amid dewdrops
of this dewdrop world
a quarrel

*

a treasure at my gate
pearls
of dew

*

into the silver dew
splashing struts
the crow

*

dewdrops scatter—
done with this crappy
world

*

simply trust! trust!
dewdrops spilling
down

*

unaware of life
passing like dewdrops...
they frolic

*

my hut—
where even beads of dew
are bent

*

looking for the bead
of dew she pinched...
a child

*

this world
is a dewdrop world
yes... but...

*

from leaf to leaf
tumbling down...
autumn dew

*

in vain grass
dewdrops forming
in vain

*

in the lightning flash
rubbing his head...
toad

*

in lightning's flash
faces in a row...
old men

*

lightning flash—
only the puppy's face
is innocent

*

lightning flash—
no way to hide
the wrinkles

*

the morning mist
tangled
in the willow

*

mountain mist—
the beautiful voice
of the dung-hauler

*

dawn—
Mount Asama's mist on the dinner tray
crawls

*

from the great bronze
Buddha's nostrils...
morning mist

*

pouring out
the hanging temple bell...
mist

*

moo, moo, moo
from the mist cows
emerge

*

mountain mist
just passing through...
big sitting room

*

night mist—
the horse remembers
the bridge's hole

*

at my house
morning mist, noon mist
evening mist

*

is that dew
the horse's tears?
autumn mountain

*

bad luck!
into the bonfire for the dead
a tiger moth

*

delighted by bonfires
for the dead...
children

*

the youngest child
on the grave visit
brings the broom

*

the old dog
leads the way...
visiting graves

*

a wrinkled face
he's my age...
lanterns for the dead

*

someone else's affair
you think...
lanterns for the dead

*

stoking it
to find my shoes...
lantern for the dead

*

one dies out
two die out...
lanterns for the dead

*

veiling the face
of the Bride Star...
nettle tree

*

don't cry, insects—
lovers part
even among the stars

*

griping about
the war lord's fireworks...
mouths of Edo

*

an arm for a pillow
fireworks boom!
ka-boom!

*

boom! boom! ka-boom!
so many duds...
fireworks

*

even one-penny
fireworks...
ooo! ahh!

*

defeated sumo wrestler—
is his father
watching too?

*

the sumo wrestler
has come from afar...
parents' grave

*

even the beggar
has a favorite
wrestler

*

sumo champion—
he won't even step
on a bug

*

sumo match—
from trees the frogs, too
cheer

*

he makes a fine
wind-break...
sumo wrestler

*

the sumo wrestler
apologizing, releases
the sparrow

*

that gentle
moon-gazing face...
a scarecrow

*

a rush of red leaves
blown against him...
scarecrow

*

scarecrows at dusk
darkening...
human faces

*

for people
and for scarecrows
the day ends

*

standing in a world
of tranquility...
the scarecrow

*

the dragonfly
settles to sleep...
on the scarecrow

*

evening falls—
me and a scarecrow
just us two

*

the village dog
suddenly disapproves...
the scarecrow

*

packing away the scarecrow
grandpa pays
his respects

*

looking younger than me
the scarecrow casts
his shadow

*

like people
an upright scarecrow
can't be found

*

draining the rice field—
a fish also
heads home

*

the cricket's song
is accompaniment...
the rice field drains

*

in the outcasts' village too
a lovely night...
pounding cloth

*

home village—
mother's cloth-pounding
faintly heard

*

my neighbor and I
have an understanding...
cloth-pounding at night

*

an owl hooting
to the beat...
pounding cloth

*

this blessing
not allowed in Paradise...
new sake

*

nagging, nagging—
the new sake
is drained

*

a little party
in the red leaves...
mountain deer

*

leasing his antler
to the cicada...
the young buck

*

the lazy buck
croons his mating call
lying down

*

mountain temple—
on the verandah
a deer cries

*

tied to the young
buck's antler...
a letter

*

they cry to each other
across a river
deer in love

*

barking—
in a village without dogs
cries of deer

*

the woodpecker
sizes it up...
my hut

*

geese at my gate
cry all you like...
no rice

*

stretching his neck
the goose peeks in
my gate

*

rice field geese—
the village's population
surges

*

the rear goose—
well, well
a sore foot

*

from today on
you are Japanese geese...
rest easy

*

don't cry, geese—
everywhere, the same
floating world

*

begging at my gate
the geese lose
weight

*

a talented one
posed on one foot...
rice field geese

*

in the wake
of the Buddhist procession...
honking geese

*

geese flying south—
the ducks at the gate
cheer them on

*

geese at my gate—
when I return
how they glare!

*

migrating birds
haven't you seen me before
in Japan?

*

the copycat sparrows
fly along...
migrating birds

*

into the snake's hole
O foolish
mouse

*

another snake
into the hole...
three roommates

*

just as you are
become Buddha!
snake in your hole

*

the old snake
toward the Western Paradise
enters his hole

*

next year
become a butterfly!
snake in his hole

*

singing all
the cool night long...
caged insect

*

green insect
and brown insect...
a duet

*

the caged insect
sings a love song
to his wife

*

in this world
among insects too...
good singers, bad singers

*

"It's cold!"
the insects' complaining
has begun

*

still singing
the insect drifts away...
floating branch

*

pointing
at the fart bug...
laughing Buddha

*

on the tip
of Buddha's nose...
a fart bug

*

will I grow old
like you?
autumn butterfly

*

autumn butterfly
on the scarecrow's sleeve
clinging

*

sunset—
the town is buzzing
with dragonflies

*

the dragonfly
dips his butt...
Sumida River

*

resting
on the big dog's head
dragonfly

*

the dragonfly goes about
his night work...
moon at the gate

*

departing for the festival
all in red
dragonfly

*

the distant mountain
reflected in his eyes...
dragonfly

*

the dragonfly
on the deer's head...
a siesta

*

the dragonfly's
steady glare...
Mount Fuji

*

a cricket
tickling my face
passes by

*

cricket—
on the young buck's antler's
tip

*

deep inside
a cricket is singing...
oven

*

on the saddle
three, four, six...
locusts

*

making love
in the withered fields...
locusts

*

when I die
guard my grave
katydid!

*

night in the hut—
a katydid forages
for food

*

gorging himself
on the cat's food...
katydid

*

inside the broom
I'm sweeping with...
a katydid

*

still no wife
his voice grows hoarse...
katydid

*

gambling in the field—
in the pot
a katydid!

*

don't crush
the dewdrop pearls!
katydid

*

turning over in bed—
move aside!
katydid

*

crawling out
the wild dog's hole...
a katydid

*

a katydid
in the scarecrow's gut
singing

*

the katydid—
even while they sell him
singing

*

atop the scripture
reader's head...
a katydid

*

the praying mantis
hangs by one hand...
temple bell

*

in grass where the wolf
shed his fur...
wildflowers

*

watered by
the village dog...
chrysanthemum

*

off in a corner
last year's champion
chrysanthemum

*

the war lord
has pull...
chrysanthemum contest

*

if it weren't for people
they'd not grow crooked...
chrysanthemums

*

the thicket's chrysanthemum
blooms
in secret

*

like me
getting plenty of sleep...
chrysanthemum

*

it too becomes food
in the secluded house...
chrysanthemum

*

nondrinkers
stay out!
gate to the chrysanthemums

*

atop the big chrysanthemum
asleep...
caterpillar

*

into morning-glories
with one shoulder bare...
holy man

*

lost
in the morning-glories
little house

*

droplets forming
on the morning-glories...
sitting still

*

my hut
with its morning-glories
a palace

*

thatched with
morning-glories
my little hut

*

in the morning-glories
peeking out...
mouse

*

in cool morning-glories
eating my rice
alone

*

the stray cat also
picks this inn...
bush clover blooming

*

is that dew
the horse's tears?
rice blossoms

*

four or five rice stalks
at my gate...
evening falls

*

the dragonfly too
folds hands in prayer...
rice blossoms

*

rice blossoms—
a large man
lost in them

*

is half of it
human sweat?
rice field dew

*

come one! come all!
the rustling
pampas grass

*

the children
pretend to be foxes...
pampas grass

*

where people
see ghosts...
field of pampas grass

*

the kittens
play house
in the pampas grass

*

mountain field—
the mouse's hole too
under red leaves

*

the nightingale struts
crunch crunch...
red leaves

*

staring at the man
burning leaves...
stone Buddha

*

taking turns
down the little waterfall...
red leaves

*

on the sleeping dog
gently, a hat...
a leaf

*

down it comes
with a frog rider...
the leaf

*

holding it
against her cheek...
the red persimmon

*

butterflies never
tire of them...
roses of Sharon

*

a babbling brook
chills the sake...
roses of Sharon

*

in the mud
after the flood, one rose
of Sharon

*

in the gloom of night
bit by bit it grows...
the gourd

*

the aging gourd
and I
cast our shadows

*

chestnuts dropping
one by one...
the night deepens

*

little chestnuts
pissed on by the horse...
shiny new

*

after great effort
picking the big chestnut...
a wormhole

*

with the boiled chestnuts
finished, so is
the conversation

*

chestnuts dropping—
even the stone Buddha
with umbrella-hat!

*

the pitter-patter
of falling chestnuts...
a rainy night

*

the pony stepping
and crunching...
chestnuts in the field

*

knocking chestnuts
out of the little garden...
thief cat!

*

it's so pretty!
so pretty!
the poison mushroom

*

for five or six people
only one...
mushroom hunting

*

even pampas grass
waves farewell, farewell...
to autumn

7 WINTER

Tenth Month
on the tenth day...
hail

*

thin wall—
from the mouse's hole
the cold

*

though I'm loving
these travels of mine...
it's cold!

*

palms
in the cooking smoke
winter cold

*

in my thatched hut
even dreaming
the cold

*

drawing words
in an old tray's ashes...
winter cold

*

merely the sight
of wolf shit...
how cold it is!

*

the old banner
flaps in a thicket
in the cold

*

drawing nearer
to the Pure Land...
life's cold winter

*

back door—
pissing scribbles
in the first ice

*

the lucky mouse
crosses then goes back...
first ice

*

my house's
only face towel
frozen stiff

*

if you cross it
cross lightly!
ice

*

under the ice
the cat's eyes follow...
crazy fish

*

the packhorse crosses
tat-a-tat...
the ice

*

on honorable Buddha's
honorable nose
an icicle

*

using his head
the high priest breaking
icicles

*

from the tip
of the field Buddha's nose...
an icicle

*

mountain temple—
with a pull-saw cutting
icicles

*

the sound of the moat
cracking...
winter moon

*

the stonecutter
chop-chops the mountain...
winter moon

*

like he's biting
the cold moon...
gargoyle

*

come in snail
and live with me...
first winter rain

*

first winter rain—
the world fills up
with haiku

*

tea is steaming
at the mountain temple...
first winter rain

*

first winter rain—
a mad dash
to the mountain house

*

she learns how to
boil water...
first winter rain

*

cold northern rain—
the fire-starter's face
smells burnt

*

winter rain—
led by a cow
to Zenko Temple

*

in winter rain
how they scowl...
the Buddhas

*

for our sake enduring
the winter rain...
stone Buddha

*

tripping over the dog
again...
night of winter rain

*

in winter rain
toward the heart of darkness...
honking geese

*

a scary sight
worse than a wolf!
winter rain leaking in

*

tucking in
the blind priest...
winter rain

*

the clams' cremation smoke
rises...
evening's winter rain

*

huddled in one house
travelers, horses...
winter rain

*

the mountain pigeon
grumbles...
winter rain

*

in the box
four or five pennies...
night of winter rain

*

winter rain—
around Basho's grave
falling down

*

my home village
in an ugly mood...
the winter rain

*

even the sparrows
are quarreling—
steady winter rain

*

seeing me home
to my hut...
the winter rain

*

the door latch
rusting scarlet...
winter rain

*

winter rain—
the lame chicken
limps away

*

cold winter sky—
where will this wandering beggar
grow old?

*

in winter wind
in three-foot wide lodgings...
my night

*

in winter wind
the pig giggles
in his sleep

*

in winter wind
a churning, churning
in my belly

*

winter wind—
behind the farmer sowing seeds
a crow

*

winter wind—
a twenty-four cent
whorehouse

*

winter wind—
a crescendo of snores
in my trashy house

*

kindly the winter wind
sweeps
my gate

*

first frost—
my teeth could crack radishes
up to last year

*

first frost—
the smiling face
of the tea master

*

on the morning frost
the blacksmith's sparks
spurting

*

young bucks
licking each other...
morning frost

*

beggar child—
even in his lap
morning frost

*

frosty night—
scratching the window, crying
banished cat

*

frosty night—
seven poor men
in a huddle

*

the first snow
softly, softly clings...
side lock of hair

*

first snowfall—
the worms in my belly
sing

*

first snowfall—
early morning at my gate
a beggar

*

"First snowfall, snowfall!"
he says
without teeth

*

in first snow
the dog goes first...
two-penny bridge

*

first snowfall—
someone has entered
the outhouse

*

first snow—
on the desktop
a snowball

*

dark night—
the first snowflakes
hit my neck

*

first snowfall—
soon to be boiled
the playful pig

*

first snowfall—
in a splendid mood
Sir Crow

*

the first snowfall
doesn't hide it...
the dog's poop

*

mountain temple—
deep under snow
a bell

*

stone still
he lets the snow fall
colt in the pasture

*

just existing
I exist...
snow flitting down

*

night snow—
in a hush people
passing

*

well here it is,
my final home?
five feet of snow

*

to my open palms
snowflakes flitting
down

*

looking delicious
the snow flitting softly
softly

*

deep snow—
on the signpost
a crow caws

*

it's a load
on the cow's head...
pile of snow

*

what a straight
piss hole!
snow at the gate

*

children eat snow
soaking
in the hot spring

*

falling snow—
the sound of snowshoes
chomp! chomp!

*

pissing
with the neighbor...
evening snow

*

on a snowy day
the temple is packed...
pigeons, sparrows

*

he's also in no mood
to sweep the snow...
scarecrow

*

lamplight flickers
in the smallpox shack...
a blizzard

*

little straw mat—
the cat comes with a coat
of snowflakes

*

into the mouth singing
"Come, hailstones!"
a hailstone

*

fall, hailstones!
with pillow on his head
a child

*

hailstones—
look! there's one
in brother's ear

*

the child hugs
her cloth monkey...
hailstorm

*

to stand pissing
while hailstones fall...
quite a feat!

*

let loose
by some god above...
hailstones

*

in the pockets
in the sleeves...
hailstones!

*

with the samisen's
plectrum sweeping up...
hailstones

*

keeping the beat
of the prayer to Buddha...
hailstones

*

my sake keg
open for business...
sleet pours down

*

distant sight—
in withered fields
a little house's lamp

*

the preacher's
hand gestures too...
withered fields

*

to the west
is Buddha's Paradise...
withered fields

*

voices in the wind
the withered field's
crows

*

all sorts of fools
moon-gaze too...
winter prayers

*

winter prayers—
a cutpurse, too
in moonlight

*

he lets me cross
his field...
night of winter prayers

*

the hut's dog is escort
to the winter
prayers

*

my grave too
will soon need his prayer...
a monk beats his bowl

*

from a straw basket
the cat's face...
by the hearth

*

secluded house—
sweeping soot
off the dog's head, too

*

my hut's soot—
going through the motions
of sweeping it

*

kindly the wind
sweeps my sooty
hut

*

corner spider
rest easy, my soot-broom
is idle

*

bamboo soot broom—
Buddha's face too
gets a smack

*

one for the dog
one for the crow...
rice cakes

*

secluded house—
three cats guard
the rice cakes

*

tree shade—
an old man pounds rice cakes
alone

*

patched
with old wastepaper
my winter coat

*

the cricket's
winter residence...
my quilt

*

hey mice
no pissing on my old
winter quilt!

*

the farting contest
begins at once...
winter quilt

*

fool cat—
yet he knows which futon
is his

*

the man who left
slept in a ball...
futon

*

temple road—
his aged mother rides
the snow sled

*

a man pulls a snow sled
a dog atop
the cargo

*

a sparrow chirping
in his lap...
snow Buddha

*

growing old too
I trust in a Buddha
of snow

*

sparrows gather
and cheer...
my snow Buddha

*

at my gate
the snow Buddha also
scowls

*

winter seclusion—
cooking a chicken
praising Buddha

*

the death bell
tolls at the temple...
winter seclusion

*

boars and bears
are my neighbors...
winter seclusion

*

no good deeds
but also no sins...
winter seclusion

*

my sinful dog
at my side...
winter seclusion

*

the slander parties
begin...
winter seclusion

*

the cricket also
moves in with me...
winter seclusion

*

a war lord
drenching wet, passes
my cozy brazier

*

more than enough
for Priest Issa...
one bag of coal

*

charcoal fire—
morning's celebration
of coughing

*

the cherry tree
that made blossom clouds
becomes charcoal

*

the charcoal kiln's smoke
puff by puff...
tranquility

*

a wood fire—
her shadow in the window
pulling thread

*

the war lord's wood fire
rises
first

*

eyeing the potato
on the banked fire...
crow

*

frozen pickle water—
my teeth
crackle

*

even snake sushi
is given a try...
winter medicine

*

even the cat
lines up for his share...
taking medicine

*

looking shameful
to the pufferfish...
people's faces

*

sitting cross-legged
a monkey joins too...
pufferfish soup

*

wind blows—
the wild boar's sleeping face
so innocent

*

scops owl—
sleeping so well
atop the pole

*

fighting the mountain wind
on foot...
a wren

*

pooping in the field—
avert your eyes
little wren!

*

thin wall—
from the mouse's hole
a wren!

*

evening plovers—
bills are due
people are crying

*

an uproar on the beach—
children
and plovers

*

the winter fly
I spare, the cat
snatches

*

there's no shame
that you totter...
old chrysanthemum

*

standing at a six-way
crossroads
in the withered grass

*

yanking radishes
one by one...
watching the clouds

*

with a just-yanked
radish
pointing the way

*

a battle royal
with radishes...
children

*

temple nuns—
it takes two
yanking the radish

*

yanking a radish
taking a tumble...
little boy

*

with a radish
driving off a deer...
his field

*

my thought
the tree would never wither
was wrong

*

the kitten holds it down
just a moment...
fallen leaf

*

stand of trees—
my head too
withered and bare

*

lacking good sense
out-of-season flowers
on the fence

*

all alone
babbling idiocies...
drinking away the year

*

the cat joins
the party...
drinking away the year

*

Kyoto—
even under bridges
drinking away the year

*

living alone—
just one bottle
for drinking away the year

*

come what may
trusting in the Buddha
the year ends

*

KOBAYASHI ISSA

a wind-chime's
empty babble ends
the year

8 HAIKU WITHOUT SEASON WORDS

moon! blossoms!
forty-nine years walking around
a waste

*

a five-inch nail—
the pine tree
is weeping

*

not yet Buddha—
the mindless old
pine

*

with a thump, thump
the turtle drags
along

*

will I be the next one
you caw over?
crows

*

joining the samurai's
company...
Sir Dog

*

the stray cat
makes Buddha's lap
her pillow

*

my dead mother—
every time I see the ocean
every time...

*

without you—
how vast
is the grove

ABOUT THE TRANSLATOR

David G. Lanoue is a professor of English at Xavier University of Louisiana. He is a cofounder of the New Orleans Haiku Society and an associate member of the Haiku Foundation. His books include a translation (*Cup-of-Tea Poems; Selected Haiku of Kobayashi Issa*), criticism (*Pure Land Haiku: The Art of Priest Issa*), and a series of "haiku novels": *Haiku Guy, Laughing Buddha, Haiku Wars* and *Frog Poet*. Some of his books have appeared in French, German, Spanish, Bulgarian, Serbian and Japanese editions. He maintains *The Haiku of Kobayashi Issa* website, for which he translated 10,000 of Issa's haiku.

15564761R00125

Made in the USA
San Bernardino, CA
30 September 2014